MY GENTLENESS, CAST VIOLENTLY ASIDE

MISCELLANEOUS POEMS

Julian Legere

BookLeaf
Publishing

India | USA | UK

My gentleness, cast violently aside

Miscellaneous poems © 2021 Julian Legere

Presentation by *BookLeaf Publishing*

Web: www.bookleafpub.com

E-mail: info@bookleafpub.com

ISBN : 9789358362268

First edition 2021

FOR BECKY

who always helps me find the eye of the

storm

ACKNOWLEDGEMENT

Being a writer was my earliest dream, and I owe it becoming a reality to far too many people to name. But key among them are Mom, Dad, Grandpa, George Connell, Fairlith Harvey, Sarah Wethered, Pam Withers, Ivan Coyote, and Bonnie Nish & Sita Carboni. Also Becky: I know I already gave you the dedication, but it's impossible to overstate my love and gratitude to you.

PREFACE

This started as an excuse to force myself to write daily, but ended up exposing a vein of messy and extremely valuable feelings. I like to think of this book as a record of my process of becoming. Becoming a grown-up poet, becoming a writer more fully than ever before, becoming at home in parts of my self and my queerness that have been inaccessible for a long time. The becoming, and the writing, will continue, but this collection is a time capsule of the beginning of that work. The poems are as eclectic and disorganized as I am, and also similarly have a hidden wholeness that I strive never to lose but also never to fully reveal, even to myself. Life, and art, are more interesting that way.

DREAMER

A dream

is a delicate

contradiction:

easily damaged,

difficult to destroy.

But lacking flesh,

its injuries are mine to bear.

Bruised by fear,

tenderness and stiffness

forbid movement

and freeze momentum.

Cut open by capitalism.

The blood only flows

away.

The weight

of "non-essential"ism

breaks my back.

But these wounds will heal.

Lacking flesh,

a dream

is more than mortal.

It nurtures me

until I am ready

to join it

in persisting.

BEHEMOTHS

Reaching giants

puncturing the sky.

Their line-bound girth,

sheathed in fibrous armour,

rupture into earth.

The surface explodes

in bulbous curves,

like rolling landscape

wrenched vertical.

Beneath,

some unfathomable apparatus

thwarts gravity:

the behemoths lean

as no others are permitted to do.

TE FITI

flick, flick

chirp

Gentle, heavy steps.

We lock eyes;

there's knowledge in yours,

intelligence,

depth.

Quick licks of the lips.

Twitching triangles

perched.

Your curiosity

inspires me.

Your patience

astounds me.

Your love

is like the ocean:

deep,

unknowable,

primal,

powerful.

Loving you back

makes mine larger,

less selfish,

more humble,

so that I can deserve you,

because you won't tolerate anything less

THE CROSSING

I've fallen through ice,

The water's grip is too tight.

Relenting seems easier than resisting.

I always trusted the ice.

It was mostly solid,

just treacherous enough to be exciting.

The ice was inevitable,

crossing it my purpose.

From a distance,

it beckoned.

It never occurred to me to resist the call,

and once I was up close,

crossing was the only option in sight.

But I must have been somewhere else,

when I saw it from that distance.

Can I go back there?

Can I look again?

Is there some other way

to the other side?

Or some other destination,

in a direction I never looked toward?

I *can* climb out,

I know my strength enough for that.

But what then?

Continue the crossing?

Continue hitting the weak points

and slipping beneath again?

There are moments of transcendence.
I encounter beauty during the crossing.

But maybe there's beauty in those other
directions, too.

And maybe I can find them
without being on the edge of death.

Or is the edge of death the only place the
beauty lives?

UNTITLED

9

I don't need you to heal my sadness.

I just need your love

to keep it company.

WYATT

I could stare at him for hours,

this small and perfect creature

who asks nothing of my heart

but accepts with perfect ecstasy

every part of of it I give.

He takes it,

whole and delicate,

yet it never leaves my hands

A GOLDEN SEA URCHIN

They label her a predator, when all she

wants to do is eat. Her needs

are so straightforward, the

world cannot fathom. With liquid spines

they fight her as she struggles for

her dignity,

but they can't even concede her

that most natural

inheritance. Beset by their resistance

all around, she limps along

recalling faintly

the time before she was defined by being

bruised

and by the violation of imaginary lines.

The trench she crawls in has become so

deep

her whole world is inside

it, and everything besides the

mud is like a fragment of a shell

she found once: emptied of vitality. She

is the same. She is

exposed

to their cold and

unforgiving gaze.

Nevertheless, she glows with grace.

She knows it's that or

die.

Denying them the satisfaction, she shivers

with determination and, knowing what's in

store if they have their way, draws her

strength to keep her soft

self alive. Just like in the broken shell, a pink

life, infinitely vulnerable, takes joy in its

flesh.

This is what she saves.

This is the gentle core of her;

if it is destroyed, she is also.

If they had her where

they want her, she

would loose a hundred cries

and become like them to beat them with

their own ungentle rules.

They'd have stopped her

from resistance, a hundred

little times.

But the light of the

moon reflects rebellion in her eyes

SUNSET

The disc has slipped away.

Gently.

No spectacular goodbye.

The light lingers

(covering the escape).

From behind,

as I watch the final blaze,

the shadow creeps in,

landing first on the broadest trees.

Eventually,

it overtakes the light

and I feel it fall on my senses

and my mind.

A flicker: a fox, black and red.

For a while longer

the sun illuminates,

but it isn't really there.

Before long,

the nightbirds start their song.

HATCHET

16

Hatchet

Curved edge bloody

Held in her steady hand

Sharpened vengeance falls on him. Hers

and theirs

ERASURE

Erasure

is my greatest fear.

I must be careful

not to envy

those who long

for anonymity.

EULOGY FOR A QUEER VENUE

18

Why is catching flames so easy?

Why is standing tall so hard?

There's no safety in the ashes,

sometimes it feels we've lost them all.

DIAMOND

I don't want to be a diamond.
Diamonds are so hard.

Their handlers are so precious,
only valuing perfection.

So don't tell me to shine,
I'll sparkle when I choose.

I don't want to be a diamond
cut to pieces for your eyes.

WORDS

Tiny nonsense

rebels against the curse

of productivity.

Where function is demanded

I deliver joy instead.

Obscure at times

and dim.

But these small spaces

for a bit of humanity

are enough.

COFFEE

A shimmer of glass.

A shine of chrome.

Vibration in my hands

and the buzzing blade.

Fragrance hits

as I scoop and dump

and pour.

Brief impatience,

then the plunge.

Finally, the steam

and the nectar of the gods.

THE JAB

Isn't it strange

That such a moment

So quiet

So small

So unassuming

Can change everything

WIND

23

Wind rustles leaves

gentle music never bothered

by whizzing cars beneath

TEA

24

Trickling liquid

Endlessly serene

A gift of herbs and stream

BALCONY GARDEN

Delicate companions

Who once were objects to me.

Stay green, my lovelies,

Stay live.

A HOME

Drowned in light, suffocated by space

Our house becomes obscure to me.

Every object, lovingly

Arranged, seems haunted now.

It waits, expectant,

Hungry, hollow.

I feel it

Swallow

Me.

A HOME. (BEFORE)

The light is warm and the air is fresh.

We have a sanctuary here;

We are our comfort from the

Sharp and disappointing

Edges of the world.

In the cushions

And the sheets

Our love

Lives.

ACHILLEAN

28

My gentleness, cast violently aside,

Nourishes my love, my lust.

It's not from passion, so I won't take in

stride

My gentleness cast violently aside.

Because a wakened longing stirs inside,

Despite demanded roughness and my spirit

left to rust,

My gentleness, cast violently aside

Nourishes my love, my lust.